Collections for Young Scholars™

STEP–BY–STEP
PRACTICE STORIES

VOLUME 2

PROGRAM AUTHORS
Carl Bereiter
Jan Hirshberg
Valerie Anderson
Ann Brown
Marlene Scardamalia
Joe Campione
Marsha Roit

CONSULTING AUTHORS
Michael Pressley
Iva Carruthers
Bill Pinkney

OPEN COURT PUBLISHING COMPANY
CHICAGO AND PERU, ILLINOIS

Cover art by Andy San Diego

Contents

About the Step-by-Step Practice Stories

The Step-by-Step Practice Stories allow your students to apply their knowledge of phonic elements to read simple, engaging texts. Each story supports instruction and review in phonic elements and incorporates elements and words that have been learned earlier.

The students can fold and staple the pages of each Step-by-Step Practice Story to make books of their own to keep and read. We suggest that you keep extra sets of the stories in your classroom for the children to reread.

For a complete discussion of reading the Step-by-Step Practice Stories with your students, see the Phonics Review Kit teacher's guide.

How to Make a Step-by-Step Practice Story book

1. Tear out the pages you need.

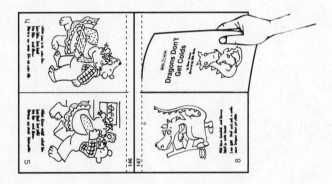

2. Place pages 2 and 7 and pages 4 and 5 face up.

3. Place pages 4 and 5 on top of pages 2 and 7.

4. Fold along the center line.

5. Check to make sure that the pages are in order.

6. Staple the pages at the staple marks.

Just to let you know . . .

Help your child discover the joy of independent reading with Open Court's *Collections for Young Scholars*. From time to time your child will bring home his or her very own Step-by-Step Practice Story books to share with you. With your help, these stories can give your child important reading practice and a joyful shared reading experience.

You may want to set aside a few minutes every evening to read these Step-by-Step Practice Stories together. Here are some suggestions you may find helpful:

- Do not expect your child to read each story perfectly, but concentrate on sharing the book together.
- Participate by doing some of the reading.
- Talk about the stories as you read, give lots of encouragement, and watch as your child becomes more fluent throughout the year!

Learning to read takes lots of practice. Sharing Step-by-Step Practice Stories is one way that your child can gain that valuable practice. Encourage your child to keep the Step-by-Step Practice Stories in a special place. This collection will make a library of books that your child can read and reread. Take the time to listen to your child read from his or her library. Just a few moments of shared reading each day can give your child the confidence needed to excel in reading.

Children who read every day come to think of reading as a pleasant, natural part of life. One way to inspire your child to read is to show that reading is an important part of your life by letting him or her see you reading books, magazines, newspapers, or any other materials. Another good way to show that you value reading is to share a Step-by-Step Practice Story with your child each day.

Successful reading experiences allow children to be proud of their new-found reading ability. Support your child with interest and enthusiasm about reading. You won't regret it!

Dan and Tracker

by Carol K. McAdam

illustrated by Anne Kennedy

Dan is a clam.
Tracker is a crab.
Dan and Tracker are pals.

1

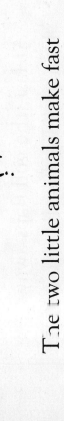

The two little animals make fast tracks in the sand.
"You are a grand crab, Tracker," says Dan.

8

Dan and Tracker have fun on the rocks.
They have fun in the sand.
Dan and Tracker make tracks in the sand.

At last, the gull flaps away.
Dan and Tracker dig out of the sand.
"We are fine now," says Tracker.
"We can play in the sand."

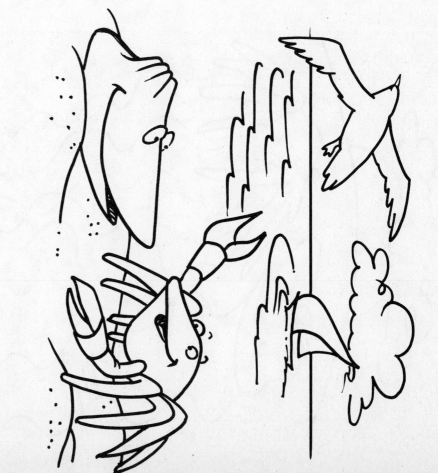

One day, a bird lands on the sand
by Tracker.
The bird is a gull.
Gulls eat crabs and clams.

The gull stops flapping and looks at
the sand.
It taps on the sand.
Where is that crab?

"Dig, Dan, dig!" calls Tracker.
Dan digs into the sand.
The gull snaps.
Dan digs faster and faster.

"Here I am, Gull!" calls Tracker.
"Can you grab me?"
The gull flaps its wings and runs
after Tracker.
The gull flaps and snaps.
Tracker begins to dig.

Scat the Cat

by Lucie Shepherd

illustrated by John Fulweiler

Ben lived on a farm.

1

"Oh well," said Ben. "I guess I have a pet. I'll call you Scat."

8

One day, Ben saw a little cat in the back pen.

Ben sat in the pen and looked at the cat. The cat looked at Ben. Then the cat sat in Ben's lap and purred.

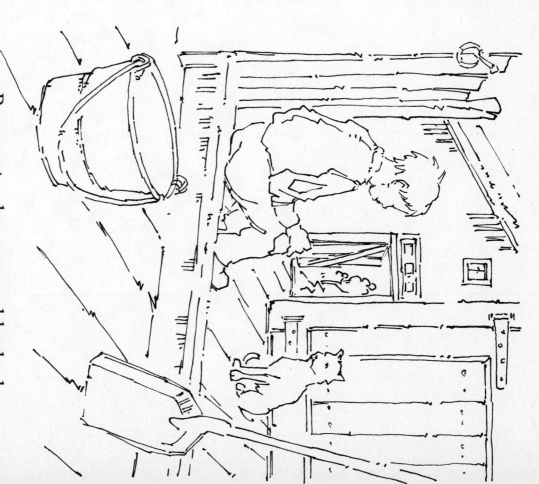

At first the cat ran when Ben went to pet him. But then Ben fed him, and he had a nap in Ben's lap.

3

When Ben went to put sand in the pen, the cat ran after a rat, and Ben fell in the pen. "Scat, cat," yelled Ben. But the cat didn't scat.

6

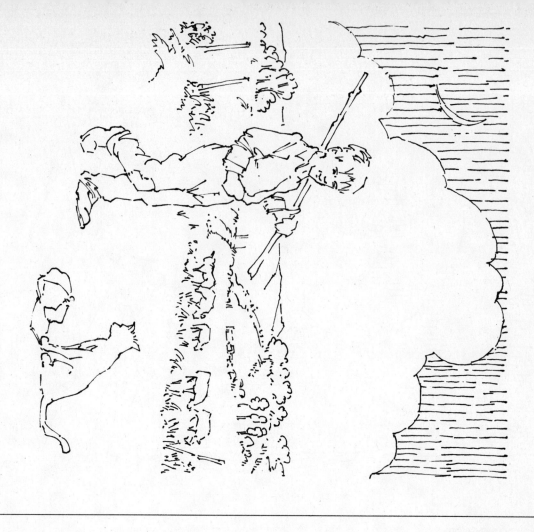

When Ben went to tend to the cows, the cat sat on Ben's cap. "Scat, cat," Ben said. But the cat didn't scat.

When Ben went to tend to the hens, the cat ran after Ben's best hen. "Scat, cat," yelled Ben. But the cat didn't scat.

Jill's Wish

by Carlos Molta

illustrated by Slug Signorino

Jill always played by the big river. She loved to fish and swim. Most of all, Jill loved digging in the sand.

1

The little girl kicked the sand. "Granting wishes just isn't my thing," she said. Then her eyes lit up. "But I do like to dig!" she said with a wink.

Jill grinned at her new pal. The little girl had granted her most important wish.

8

When children visited, Jill showed them the shells and bits of dishes she found in the river. "You should try to dig," Jill always said. The other children were not interested.

"I will try again," said the little girl.

"Think of an *important* wish."

"Well," said Jill, "then I'll wish for a pal who wants to dig with me."

The little girl put her finger to the tip of her chin. She skipped in a circle, but nothing happened.

So Jill had to dig by herself. One day Jill dug up a little bottle. She lifted the bottle out of the sand. Jill patted it with a rag.

Suddenly, a little girl was in front of Jill.

3

"I will try again," said the little girl. "Think of a better wish."

"Well," said Jill, "then I wish for a huge fishing boat."

"In a jiffy!" said the little girl. She put her finger to her lips. A huge fish fell into Jill's hands.

6

"Who are you?" asked Jill.

"Who do you think?" asked the little girl.

"Aladdin's genie? Cinderella's fairy godmother?"

"Something like that," giggled the little girl. "Make a wish!"

"Are you kidding?" gasped Jill.

"Not a bit! Think of a wish!" insisted the little girl.

"Well," said Jill, "then I wish for a million dollars."

"In a jiffy!" answered the little girl. She put her finger to the tip of her nose. A million bricks fell into the sand.

Ron's Jobs

by Alvaro Ruiz

illustrated by Robert Byrd

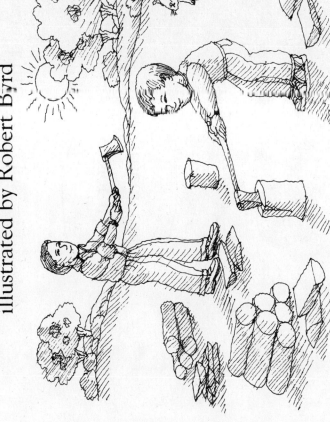

Ron and his dad chopped logs with axes. They chopped in the hot sun. Ron got ten dollars for his bank. "This is not a lot of fun," Ron said.

1

"Just wait, Pop," he would say. "Someday, I'll have an idea that is not odd."

"Don't stop having odd ideas, Ron," his pop would tell him as he got the ax. "But don't stop chopping logs yet."

8

Ron was always looking for a new job.

"Just wait, Pop," Ron would say. "Someday I'll be rich."

Sometimes, just walking along, Ron would think of a job.

I've got it! Corncob dolls!

And even when the job was a flop, Ron still was not bothered.

"It was an oddball idea," he would say. "Another job will come along."

When the job did not work out,
Ron was not mad.
"It was an oddball idea," he would
say. "Another job will come along."

Step-by-Step Practice Story 4   © 1995 Open Court Publishing Company

Often, it seemed like a job idea was
right in his hands all along.

I've got it!
Pop bottle mailboxes!

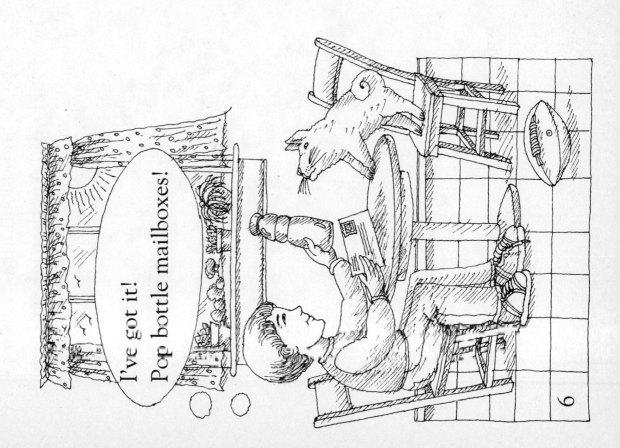

Sometimes job ideas seemed to drop with a plop from the sky.

I've got it! I'll collect lost golf balls!

4

But when a job hit rock bottom, Ron was not upset. "It was an oddball idea, anyway," he would say. "Another job will come along."

5

Skunks Have Fun!

by Carolyn Crimi
illustrated by Nelle Davis

Pug and Fudge were two small skunks. They slept under a stump in the forest. One day Pug and Fudge couldn't think of anything to do. "I know!" said Pug. "Let's scare all the other animals!"

1

Pug and Fudge rushed home. Their fun was over. But the other animals all had a good chuckle!

8

Pug and Fudge hid behind a plum tree. They waited until they saw a chipmunk run by. "BOO!" yelled the skunks. The chipmunk jumped and ran away.

"That was fun!" said Pug. "Let's do it again!"

"You have upset the animals," grunted the monster. "You must never play such a trick again! Do you understand?"

"Yes. Yes." muttered Pug and Fudge.

This time they hid until a slug crept by. "BOO!" yelled Pug and Fudge. The stunned slug ducked under a rock.

"That was fun, too!" said Pug. "Let's do it again!"

3

Suddenly, a monster jumped in front of Pug and Fudge.

"Are you the skunks who scared the animals?" thundered the monster.

"Uh . . . uh . . . ," stammered Pug and Fudge. The two skunks were too scared to talk.

6

Pug and Fudge spent all afternoon scaring animals. Finally Pug said, "This is fun, but I'm getting sleepy."

"So am I," said Fudge. "Let's rest for a bit."

Pug and Fudge snuggled up under the plum tree and slept. When they got up, it was dark.

"This isn't fun," said Pug. "We'd better run home!"

The Peddler and His Donkey

by Carolyn Crimi

illustrated by Julie Durrell

Once upon a time there was an old peddler named Casper. He was very poor, but he had a grand donkey called Chip. Casper loved Chip very much.

1

"Well, Chip," said Casper. "We have no silver, but I'd much rather be a poor man with you than a rich man without you!"

8

One day, on the way home, Casper and Chip stumbled upon a pot of silver in a ditch by the path. "Look, Chip!" said Casper, looking at the silver. "This silver will make me a rich man!" Casper put the silver in Chip's bag and went on.

2

Chip still did not get up. Casper took the silver box off his back. "There, Chip!" said Casper. "There is nothing left on your back. I will help you get up."

Chip got up. Then Chip and Casper crossed the river to home.

7

In a little bit, Casper and Chip
stumbled upon a silver rock as big as a
man's hat. "Look, Chip!" said Casper.
"This rock will make me a rich man!"
Casper put the rock in Chip's bag.
The rock was heavy. Poor Chip
plodded along.

3

Chip still could not get up. Casper
took the silver rock out of his bag.
"There, Chip!" said Casper. "Now
can you get up?"

6

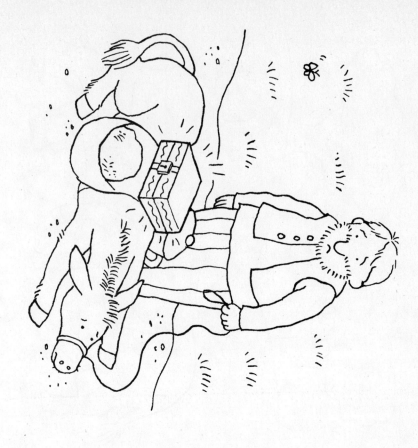

A little later, Casper and Chip stumbled upon a solid silver box.

"Look, Chip!" said Casper. "This box will make me a rich man!"

Casper lifted the box onto Chip's back. But the box was too heavy. Poor Chip fell to the ground.

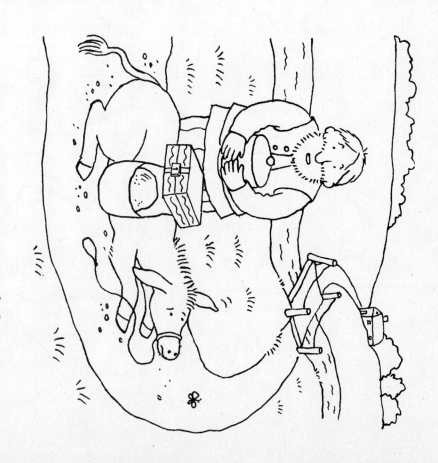

"Get up, Chip!" cried Casper. "We must cross the river to get this silver home!" But Chip could not get up. Casper took the pot of silver out of Chip's bag.

"There, Chip!" said Casper. "Now can you get up?"

A Gift for the Queen

by Carolyn Crimi
illustrated by Roz Schanzer

Once there was a queen with three girls. Their names were Martha, Arlene, and Carla.

"Tomorrow is my birthday," said the queen to the girls. "The girl who finds the smartest and most thoughtful gift will be the next queen."

1

Then Carla gave the queen her scarf.

"This," said the queen, "will keep me warm, and yellow is a charming color! You will be a smart queen, Carla."

And Carla was.

8

The two oldest girls, Martha and Arlene, worried. "There is a party in the park tonight!" they said. "We must get a gift quickly or we will miss the party!"

"The market is not far," said Martha. "I will run and buy Mother a sparkling cart."

2

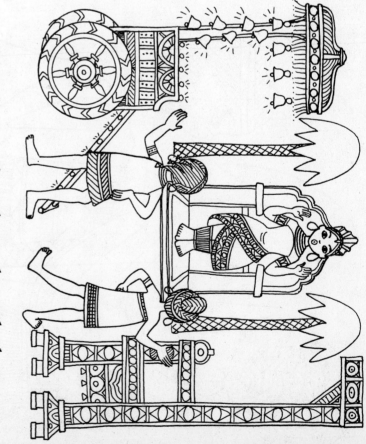

The next day, the girls took their gifts to the queen.

"Here is a lovely cart," said Martha. "See how it sparkles!"

"This marble throne is the largest in the kingdom by far!" said Arlene.

"These are very charming," said the queen, "but I already have a cart and a throne."

7

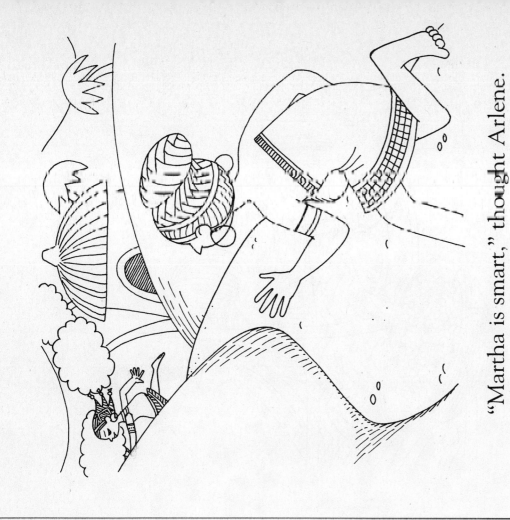

"Martha is smart," thought Arlene. "I will run to the market, too. I will buy Mother a marble throne. It will be larger than Martha's cart. Mother will think I am the smartest, and I won't miss the party!"

3

Carla worked hard on the scarf. By dark, her arms hurt, but the scarf still wasn't finished.

"I will work far into the night," she said.

"You are a silly girl," said Martha and Arlene. "Think of missing a party for a silly scarf."

6

The youngest girl, Carla, thought hard about her mother's gift. She said, "I will make a scarf." Carla bought yards of yellow yarn at the market and started to work.

Carla's sisters argued with her. "Our gifts are far more charming," they said. "You will have to work hard. You will miss the party!"

The Most Wonderful Home

by Dottie Raymer
illustrated by Paige Billin-Frye

A beaver named Burt built himself a wonderful home in the river.

"This is the most wonderful home that has ever been built," said Burt Beaver.

1

Now Burt Beaver and Oliver Otter work and play hard together every day. And all the other river animals agree that Burt and Oliver have the most wonderful home that has ever been built.

8

One day, an otter named Oliver built a slippery mud slide in the ferns next to Burt Beaver's home.

"Oliver Otter's home is better than mine," thought Burt. "I was here first! I must make my home better than that otter's!"

Oliver turned to Burt in surprise. "I wish that I could make a home like yours," he said. "but I can't. My tail isn't sturdy enough!"

Burt and Oliver looked at their tails. "We are both hard workers," they said. "Maybe we can work together!"

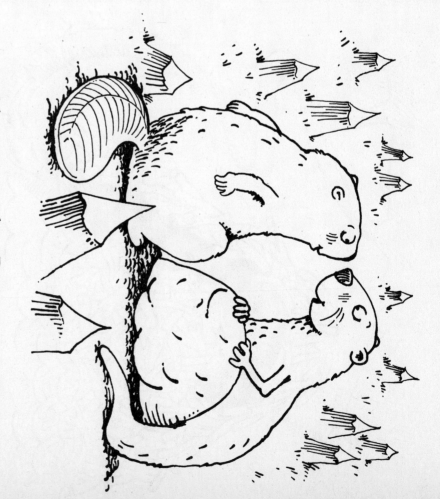

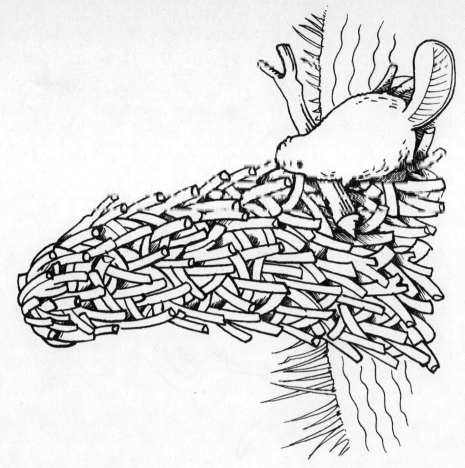

Burt Beaver made his home stronger and bigger with dirt and sticks.

"Now my home is the most wonderful home that has ever been built," said Burt firmly.

3

Poor Burt Beaver *was* very surprised when he saw Oliver Otter's wonderful home. But he was also tired.

"I wish I could build a longer, slippery mud slide like yours," he told Oliver, "but I can't. My tail isn't slippery enough."

6

After Oliver Otter saw Burt's wonderful home, he returned to his slippery but simple mud slide.

"Burt Beaver thinks he has the better home, but I can make my home even better," thought Oliver. He hurried off to start work.

Soon, Oliver Otter had built an even longer, better mud slide through the ferns.

"What a surprise Burt Beaver will have when he sees this!" smirked Oliver. "This is truly the most wonderful home that has ever been built."

Brave Dave

by Ana Rojas

illustrated by George Ulrich

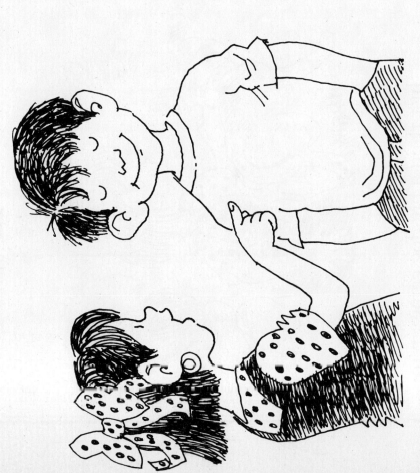

1

"You're brave, Ada," said Dave.

"Yes, Dave," said Ada, "But will I ever be as brave as you?"

8

"I am the bravest!" Dave said.

"I swam across a lake to save a baby."

"But Dave," said his little sister Ada, "you can't swim."

2

Just then a big dog came up to Dave and Ada.

"I hate big dogs!" said Dave.

"Scram, dog, scram!" yelled Ada. She chased the dog.

7

"I chased a lion in Africa," said Dave.

"But Dave," said Ada, "you are scared of cats."

3

"I raced a truck on a racetrack," said Dave.

"But Dave," said Ada, "you can't race."

6

"I saved a snake from a dragon," said Dave.

"But Dave," said Ada, "you hate snakes."

"I traded bananas with the apes," said Dave.

"But Dave," said Ada, "you hate bananas."

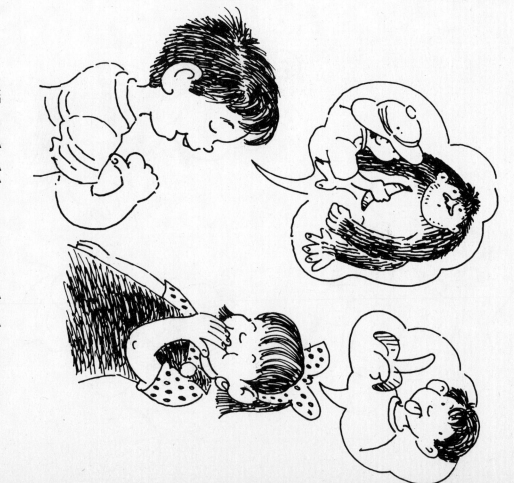

43

Step-by-Step 10 Practice Story

Jay's Pail

by Michelle Chang
illustrated by Kate Flanagan

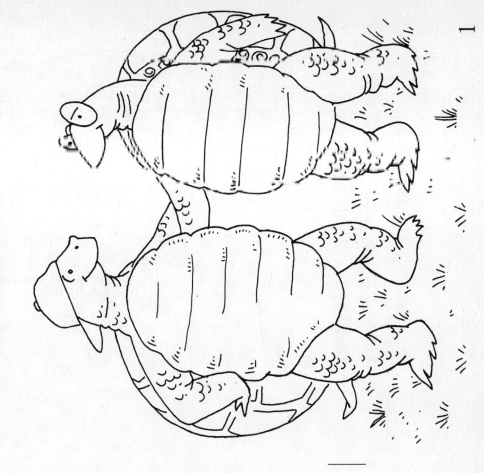

1

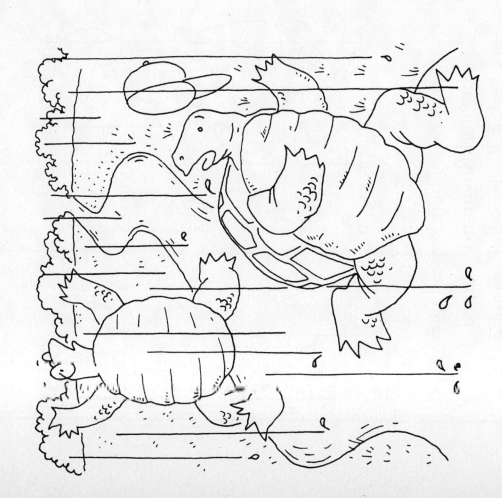

BOOM! Another big crash came. Jay looked at Raymond. Raymond looked at Jay. Then they both raced down the trail.

8

On his way to the park, Jay picked up a new pail. It was painted red with yellow fishes, green shells, and blue snails.

BOOM! There was a big crash. Jay and Raymond jumped. Jay looked at Raymond. Raymond looked up.

"I am not afraid," whispered Jay.

"Then I am not afraid," said Raymond.

"Hurray!" said Jay. "I can play with this pail today." He ran down the trail.

3

SPLASH! The rain started. It fell fast and hard. The pail filled with rain water. The sand turned to mud. But Jay and Raymond were not afraid.

6

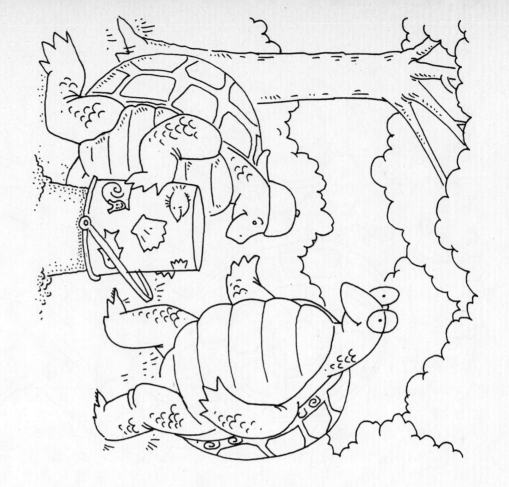

Jay took his pail to the sand under the trees. He started playing with his friend Raymond.

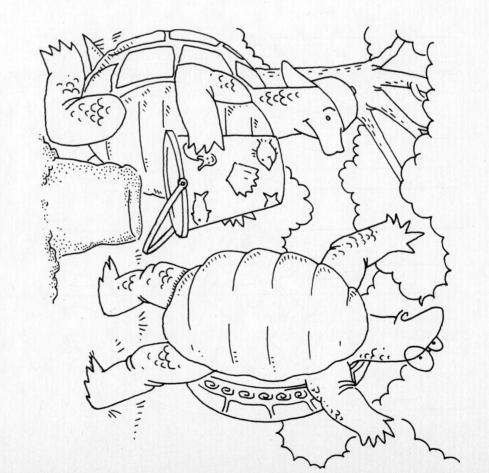

"Wait!" yelled Raymond. "It may rain!"

"I'm not afraid of the rain," said Jay.

"Then I'm not afraid of the rain," said Raymond.

The Animal Game

by Wiley

illustrated by Ellen Joy Sasaki

It was raining. The wind whipped the branches back and forth. Steve, Pete, and Eve had nothing to do.

1

Just then Pete and Steve heard the buzz of the hornet. Pete, Steve, and Eve ran upstairs and hid under the bed.

"Maybe we can play another game," said Eve.

Pete and Steve agreed.

8

"Let's play the animal game," said Eve.

"The animal game?" asked Steve and Pete. "How do you play it?"

It was Eve's turn. She put her hands in the air. She waved them back and forth. She jumped up and down. She looked mad.

"Are you a bird?" asked Steve.

"Are you a rabbit?" asked Pete.

"No!" yelled Eve. "There is a hornet after me!"

"You just pretend to be an animal. Don't tell what animal you are. Keep it a secret. Then we have to tell what you are," explained Eve.

3

"Are you a rat?" asked Pete.
"No!" giggled Steve.
"Are you a pig?" asked Eve.
"No!" cried Steve. "I'm an elephant!"

6

"Okay," said Pete. "Let me go first."
Pete started walking with his hands on
the rug. He looked silly.
"Are you a cat?" asked Eve.
"No," said Pete.
"Are you a dog?" asked Steve.
"No," said Pete. "I'm a zebra."

"You're next Steve," Pete said.
"I know what I'll be!" Steve said.
Steve began stomping on the rug.
His head swayed back and forth.
He looked scary.

Sleepy Keefer

by Peter Matheny

illustrated by Joyce Audy Zarins

Sleepy Keefer was scared. Down the street he ran. He ran under big feet. He ran into a big building and hid beneath a heap of sticks.

"I am free!" Keefer squeaked. "But I am so sleepy! I need to find a place to sleep!"

1

"Why won't he speak?" wondered Keefer. "Perhaps he's sleepy, too."

"I know just how you feel," squeaked Keefer sleepily. Keefer climbed up the dinosaur and made a neat nest. "Pleased to meet you," whispered Keefer. And the two new friends settled into a deep peaceful sleep.

8

Sleepy Keefer peeked out from behind the sticks. "Eeek!" he squeaked. All Keefer could see was sticks. Big sticks. Little sticks. Sticks that stood very tall. Keefer could feel his heart beat very fast.

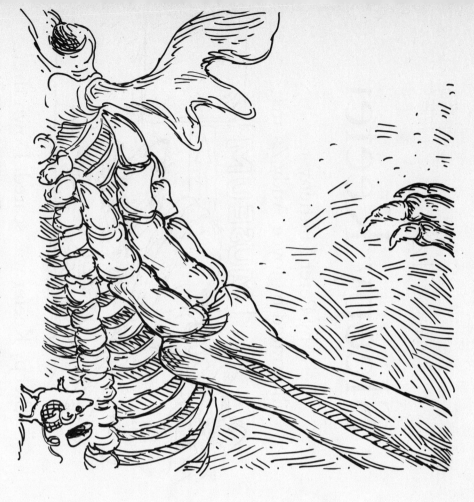

Then Keefer saw a sign near the sticks. "Dinosaur?" squeaked Keefer. "These sticks are a dinosaur!" exclaimed Keefer.

"Do dinosaurs eat mice?" Sleepy Keefer asked. The dinosaur did not speak.

"Do dinosaurs sweep?" Sleepy Keefer asked.

The dinosaur still did not speak.

Sleepy Keefer began to sneak past the sticks. "Eeek!" he squeaked. All he could see were feet. Big feet. Little feet. Feet everywhere. Keefer hid his head.

"I'm too sleepy for this," whispered Keefer. Keefer leaned back and fell asleep where he was.

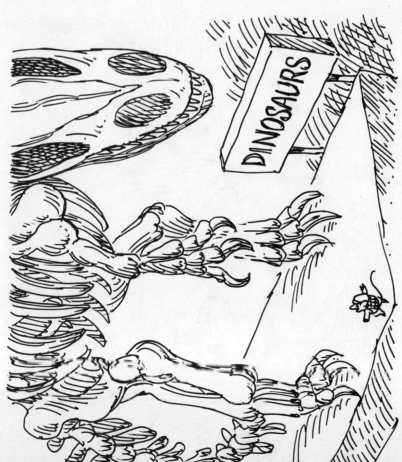

Keefer crept out from beneath the sticks. He peeked back. The sticks seemed to have grown! Keefer crept a bit farther. He peeked back again.

"Please tell me what you are," Keefer squeaked to the sticks. But the sticks did not speak.

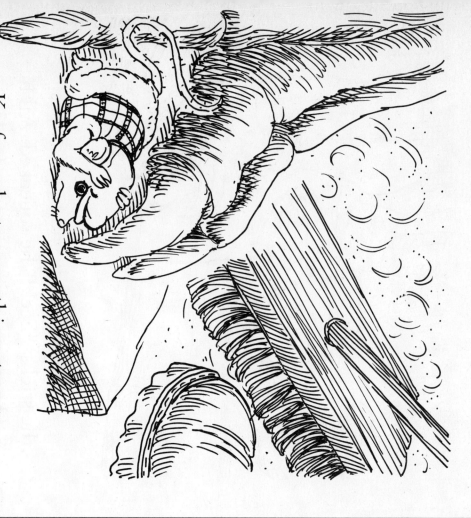

Keefer woke to something strange. A man was pushing a broom—sweep, sweep, sweep. Keefer hid beneath the sticks. "I don't like things that sweep!" mumbled Keefer. The man did not see Keefer.

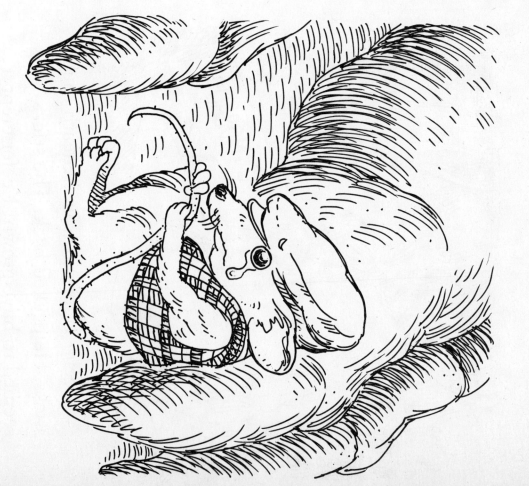

A big tear slid down Keefer's cheek. "All I need is a peaceful place to sleep!" he cried. "But how will I ever find it? All I can see is sticks!"

Taffy for Uncle Billy

by Marie Foster

illustrated by Andy San Diego

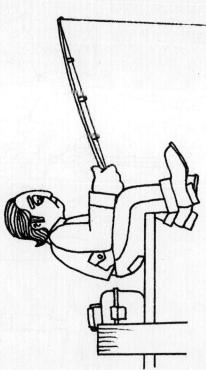

Uncle Billy was a sad man. Every day, he walked to the end of the pier to fish. Uncle Billy never really got anything. He just sat there and looked sad.

1

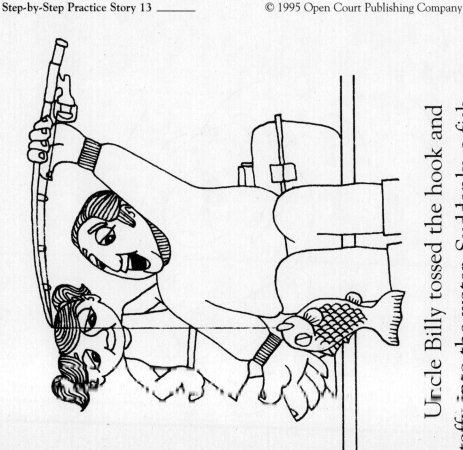

Uncle Billy tossed the hook and taffy into the water. Suddenly, a fish jumped up and grabbed the hook.

"I've got one! I've got one!" yelled Uncle Billy. "At last!"

Terry grinned at her happy uncle.

"Yes," she said. "A good piece of taffy can do anything!"

8

Everybody wanted to be friendly to Uncle Billy. But Uncle Billy just sat sadly. Everybody began to think that Uncle Billy was angry. Finally, everybody stopped being friendly.

2

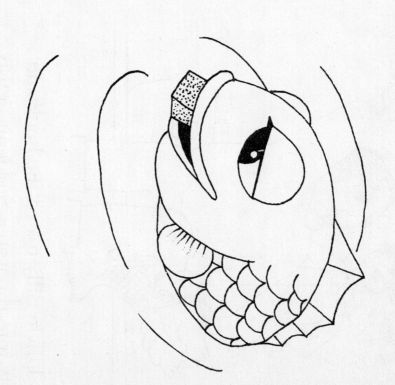

One day, during a really good story, Terry dropped a piece of taffy into the muddy water. A fish snatched the taffy and quickly swam away. Uncle Billy stared at the fish. Then he stuck a piece of taffy onto his fish hook.

7

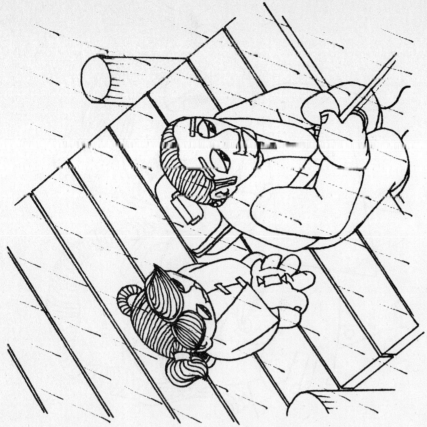

Uncle Billy's niece, Terry, worried about him. Every day, she watched him on the pier. One chilly, rainy day, Terry walked to the end of the pier.

"Look what I have, Uncle Billy! Taffy! Your favorite candy!" she called.

Uncle Billy didn't say anything.

3

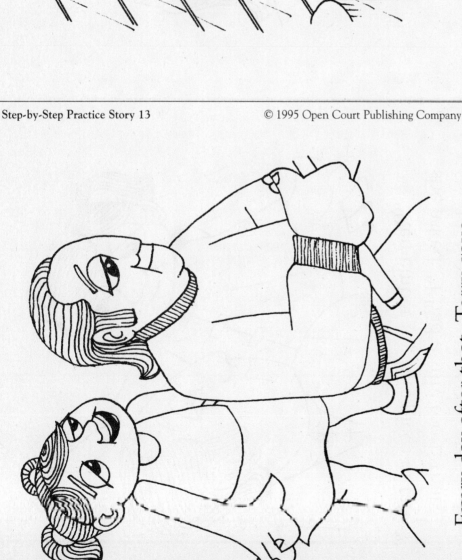

Every day after that, Terry gave her uncle pieces of taffy. Every day, she shared more stories with him. Her uncle sat silently eating and fishing. Sometimes he grinned, but he never said anything. And he never got any fish.

6

"Have some, Uncle. It tastes wonderful!" said Terry. Before Uncle Billy could shake his head, Terry popped a piece of the taffy into his mouth. Uncle Billy silently ate the taffy.

As her uncle ate, Terry told him a funny story.

"Remember my first piece of taffy?" she asked. "I had a silly tooth that wouldn't come out. You said a good piece of taffy would get my tooth out. You said a good piece of taffy could do anything."

The story made Uncle Billy grin. Terry hadn't seen him grin in a very long time.

Be a Rock Collector

by Carolyn Crimi

illustrated by Barbara Bruno

Have you ever picked up a rock just because you liked the way it looked?

1

So the next time you are walking, you might just find the rock that will make you a rock collector for life!

8

Was it dull or shiny? Heavy or light? If you like looking at rocks, you might be a rock collector. Rock collectors are people who like rocks.

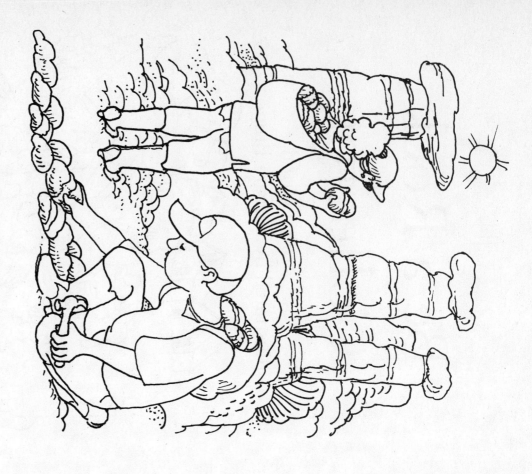

Rocks are not just for studying. Small rocks can be painted with smiling faces or made to look like tiny mice. Two large rocks might make a nice set of bookends. A giant rock might be just the right size for climbing.

Rocks are everywhere. You might find rocks by rivers. You might find them on the beach. You might even find them along a city street.

3

When you find an interesting rock, check the library for books about rocks. Books can tell you what kind of rock you have. Write the name of the rock on a slip of paper. Then paste the paper and the rock on the inside of the lid of a small box.

Surprise! You have started a rock collection!

6

There are different kinds of rocks. Some rocks, like limestone, are quite soft. These rocks easily break into tiny bits. Others, like quartzite, are hard.

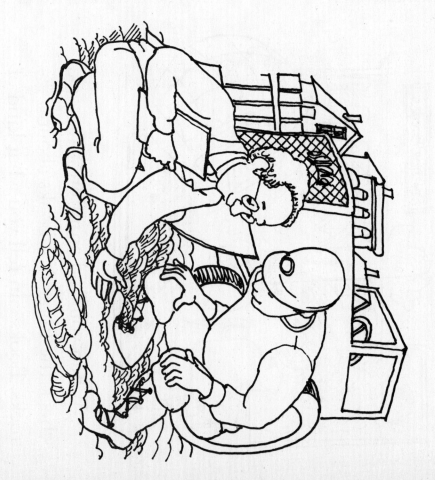

Rocks with fossils are highly prized. These rocks contain the remains or marks from plants and animals that were alive long ago. Fossils turn up in the most surprising places. Keep your eyes open. You might find one, too!

The Sly Fox and the Shy Bird

by Wiley

illustrated by Kate Flanagan

Once a sly fox lived deep in the forest. The sly fox was very hungry. No matter how hard he tried, he could not find anything to eat.

"I might die of hunger," he cried.

1

"See fox," said the shy bird, "you are shy, but not as sly as I."

"Good-bye, sly fox!" cried the bird, and she flew off into the sky.

8

One day, the sly fox spied a bird flying in the sky.

"I will try to trick this bird," said the sly fox. "It will make a nice fried bird pie."

"Oh, shy little bird," called out the sly fox. "You look tired. Come and lie on my soft fur."

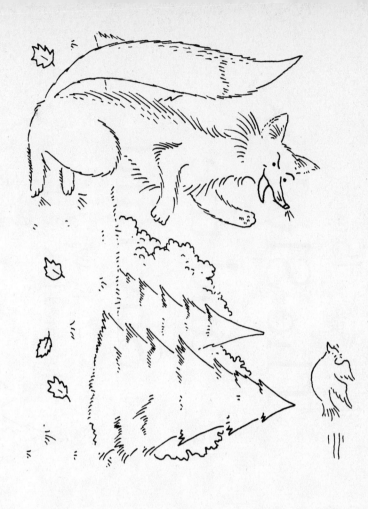

Quickly, the shy bird tied the fox's nose to the box.

"My nose is stuck!" grumbled the fox. "I can't pry it loose!"

The bird in the sky didn't say anything.

"Why don't you reply?" asked the sly fox.

"Oh," cried the bird, "I am too shy to talk to you."

"_ will try to help you," replied the shy bird. "I will try to tie the string."

The bird flew down from the sky.

"Hold the string down with your long nose while I tie it," she said to the fox.

"Sweet, shy bird," said the sly fox.
"I need your help to tie this string
around my pie box. Inside is a yummy
fried pie for my mother."

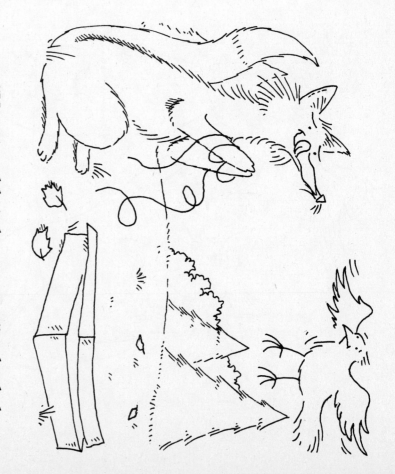

"You wouldn't lie to me?" asked the
shy bird.

"Oh, no," cried the sly fox as he
licked his lips. "I need your help."

"I'll bet there is no fried pie in
that box," the shy bird mumbled.
"I'll bet that sly fox wants me to be the
fried pie!"

Prince Otto's Wish

by Carlos Molta

illustrated by Sucie Stevenson

1

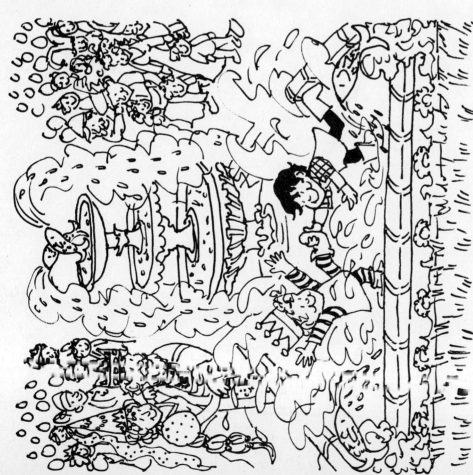

So all in the kingdom came to see
that gifts alone just could not be.
For when the story reached its end,
Otto's only wish was for a friend.

8

Little Prince Otto awoke each day
with nothing to do but play.
But did he smile? Oh no, not he.
Prince Otto was alone, you see.

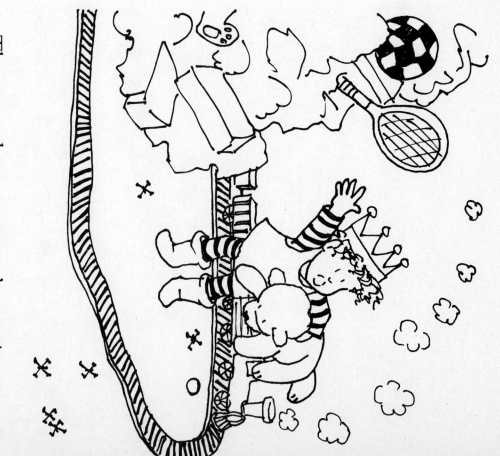

Then, much to everyone's surprise,
the prince himself spoke words so wise.
"Toys alone cannot bring a smile.
They must be shared, not heaped in
  a pile."

"Otto, what is it you need?"
his mother said, "I'll grant any deed.
I'll tie the sun with ropes of gold,
and place it in your hands to hold."

3

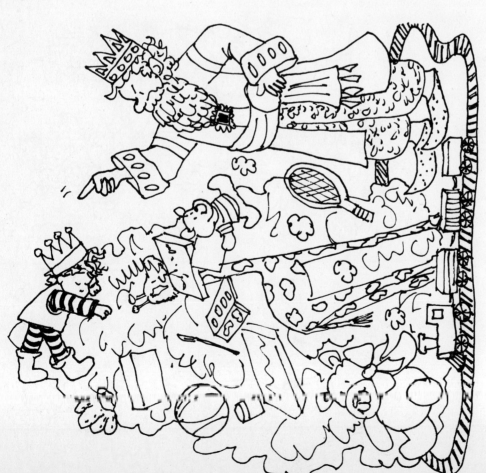

The king sent Otto toys and more,
but they just made young Otto snore.
The king glared, and began to scold,
"Prince Otto, how can you be so bold?"

6

But little Otto chose to mope,
and left his mom with no hope.
"Oh dear," she said, "What can I do?
My riches and more I'd give to you."

4

Aunts and uncles sent Otto roses.
Jesters told jokes and wore red noses.
Servants gave Otto candy and clothes,
but Otto said, "Please! No more of
those!"

5

Chinlow's Talent

by Jo Olson

illustrated by Jean & Mou-sien Tseng

1

Finally, the emperor called Chinlow to him. "Show me," he said. Chinlow looked into the face of a tiny rose. The rose grew and became lovely. Then the emperor said to Chinlow, "Now look at me."

Chinlow looked into the emperor's eyes. The emperor saw love in her eyes. "Now I know her talent," he said, "but I am not afraid of it. Her talent is love."

8

In the little village of Singboat lived a girl named Chinlow. She loved all things of nature. All things of nature loved her.

The birds of the forest sang more sweetly for her. The snows on the hills shone whitest for her.

2

Each time Chinlow looked into the face of a tiny rose. Each time the Chinlow looked at began to grow and grow until it became the loveliest rose in its garden row.

Each time, the teacher said, "I saw her talent, but I do not know it."

7

The roses Chinlow planted would always grow tall. The stream flowed and sparkled brighter when she walked by its side.

"Where does Chinlow's talent come from?" people of the village asked. "Even the rainbow is more dazzling over Chinlow's home."

3

The emperor wanted to find out about Chinlow's secret talent. He called for his wisest teachers. Teachers came and knelt low before the emperor. "I must know," he said, "the talent of this lowly Chinlow."

One by one the teachers spoke to Chinlow. "Show me," each teacher said.

6

Slowly stories of Chinlow's mighty talent began to grow. The stories seemed to blow from village to village with the gentle breezes. They fell from the sky with each soft raindrop.

People began to ask, "How can we know the talent of Chinlow?"

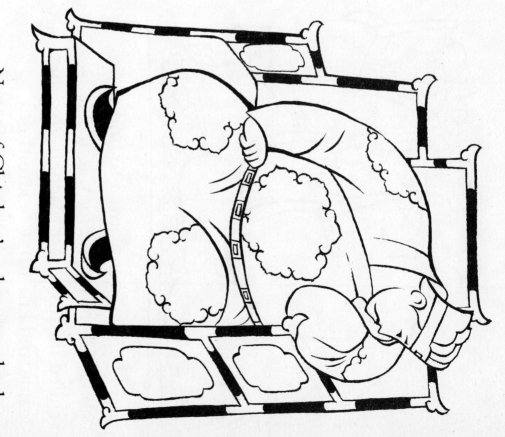

News of Chinlow's talent reached the emperor in far away Pancoat.

"Could the talent of a simple child overthrow an emperor?" he wondered. "I must not let this go on."

Mrs. Music Goes for a Walk

by Carolyn Crimi

illustrated by NeLe Davis

Every day Mrs. Music and her cat Rescue went for a walk.

"Look!" Mrs. Music said one day to Rescue. "Someone has thrown a beautiful dish into the trash. That dish would look grand on my table."

1

The next day Mrs. Music and Rescue went for their walk.

"Oh, my!" said Mrs. Music when she saw the bugle. "Rescue, look at that beautiful bugle! I wonder where I can put it?"

8

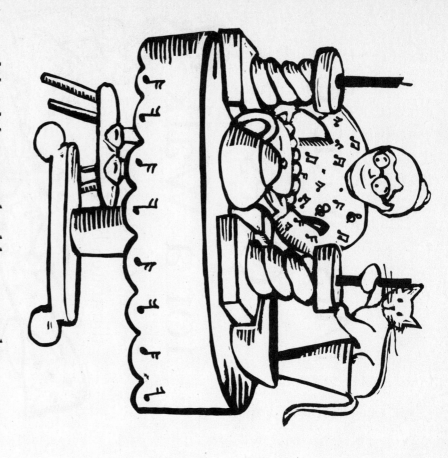

Mrs. Music rushed home and put the dish on her table. The dish looked beautiful, but the table was full.

"Rescue," said Mrs. Music, "a good cleaning is needed! I don't use these candlesticks anymore. I will throw them away."

Mary hurried home with the uniform. The uniform did look beautiful, but Mary's closet was full.

"A good cleaning is needed," Mary said. "I don't use this bugle anymore. I will throw it away."

Hugo was walking home from work when he saw the candlesticks.

"What unusual candlesticks!" he said to himself. "They must have come from a museum. Aunt McCube would love them!"

Hugo picked up the candlesticks and took them to his aunt.

3

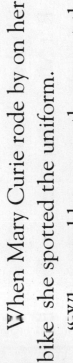

When Mary Curie rode by on her bike she spotted the uniform.

"Why would anyone throw out this great musician's uniform?" she cried.

"It's such a popular color! I will take it home."

6

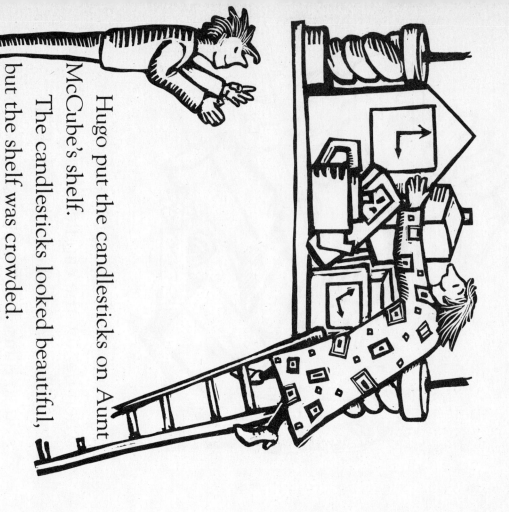

Hugo put the candlesticks on Aunt McCube's shelf.

The candlesticks looked beautiful, but the shelf was crowded.

"Nephew," said Mrs. McCube, "a good cleaning is needed! I don't use this clock anymore. I have quite a few others. I will throw this one away."

Later that day Mr. Fuel came by with his mule cart. "What a beautiful clock!" he cried. "It must be valuable. I will take it home."

But Mr. Fuel's mule cart was full.

"A good cleaning is needed," Mr. Fuel said to his mule. "This old uniform is not a popular color. I will throw it away."

Amazon Day

by Dottie Raymer
illustrated by Diane Elasius

It is a peaceful day in the Amazon.
A light breeze shakes the tree leaves.

1

In the trees above, only the three-toed sloth remains quiet. It moves so slowly that mold grows on its fur. The green mold helps it hide in the leaves. The sloth isn't moving at all. The lazy sloth is asleep. When night comes, it will slowly wake to eat.

8

High above the jungle, a huge eagle watches as the rain forest wakes up. So far, the day seems still.

Suddenly, monkeys screech and parrots take flight. A jaguar slips silently through the trees below. The jaguar's spotted coat hides it well. It stops beside a stream and dips its tail into the water. A fish rises to the bait. Surprise! The jaguar has a tasty meal.

But the rain forest is never completely quiet. Deep in the jungle, creatures stir. Spider monkeys leap from tree to tree. Their tails grab long vines as they find their way to ripe fruits.

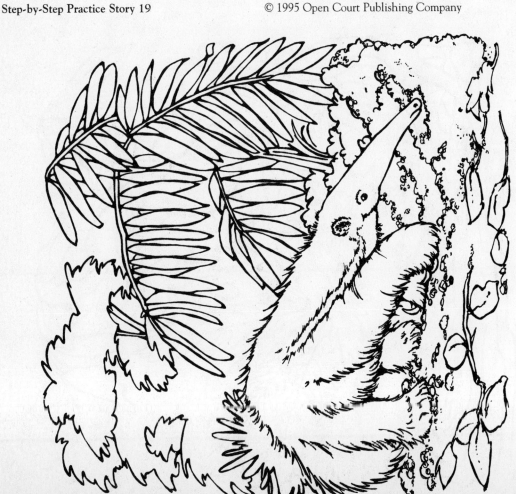

Nearby, a giant anteater uses its claws to open an ant nest. It pokes its long nose into the nest to find its tiny food.

A bird perches in a fig tree. It uses its bright beak to snip off a fig. It throws the fig into the air. It catches the fig in its beak, and lets it roll down its throat.

Below the bird, a snake sneaks up on a huge lizard. Just in time, the giant lizard slides quietly into a stream and escapes.

Scooter and Tooter

by Marie Foster

illustrated by George Ulrich

Scooter and Tooter lived in an old boot next to a pool. Most of the time, Scooter's and Tooter's lives went smoothly. During the day, they snoozed inside the cool boot. At night, they snooped for food or scooted around the pool.

1

Now, whenever Hunter is hungry, Scooter scoots into his old boot and makes a big pot of root stew. Hunter is never in a bad mood. And the mice are free to snoop for food, even when the moon shines!

8

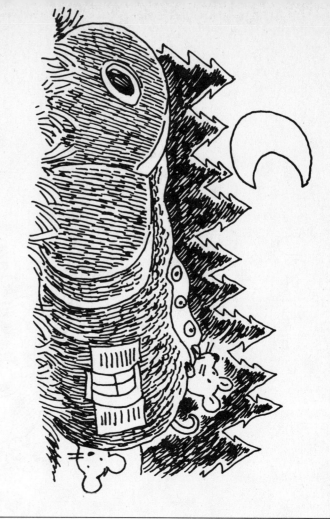

The only time Scooter's and Tooter's lives didn't go smoothly was when the moon shone. When the moon shone, they did not snoop for food or scoot around the pool. They hid in the boot and listened for Hunter's "Hoot, hoot, hoot." "Hoot, hoot, hoot" meant that Hunter was hungry. The mice were not safe when Hunter was hungry.

Hunter's hooting got closer and closer. "He's really in a bad mood tonight," said Tooter. "He must *hate* root stew!"

Scooter listened hard. Then he squeaked with glee! "Why, Hunter isn't calling 'Hoot, hoot, hoot!'" he exclaimed. "Hunter is calling 'Stew, stew, stew!'"

All of the mice brooded about Hunter.

"If we don't do something soon," they squeaked, "Hunter will surely swoop down and catch one of us."

3

Scooter scooted back to his boot.

As the moon rose, Scooter and Tooter listened. In the distance, they heard Hunter's call. "Hoot, hoot, hoot! Hoot, hoot, hoot!"

"Rats!" said Scooter gloomily. "He didn't like the root stew!"

6

While the others brooded, Scooter thought about Hunter.

"Hunter always seems hungry," he said, "and he always seems to be in a bad mood. Maybe Hunter isn't getting anything good to eat. If I ate what he eats, I'd be in a bad mood, too."

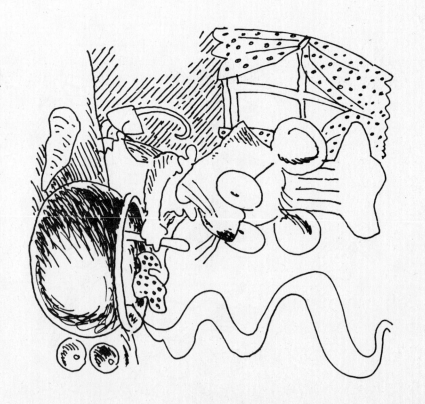

The next day while the others slept, Scooter worked. Into a pot, he tossed chopped roots, berries, and flower shoots. That night, before the moon rose, Scooter crept over to Hunter's roost. There, he left a big bowl of root stew.

Step-by-Step 2 | Practice Story

Old Hook

by Carolyn Crimi

illustrated by Andy San Diego

Once an old man lived by a brook in the woods. Whenever the children played by the brook, the old man would yell, "Stay away from my brook!" The children called the man Old Hook.

1

The day Lucy finished reading *Peter Pan*, Lucy felt sad. "I'll miss reading," she told Old Hook.

"You need more practice," said Old Hook. "Bring another book."

Now Lucy reads to Old Hook every day. And if they have time, Lucy and her mother sometimes even play in the brook.

8

Lucy always looked sadly at Old Hook. "Why won't he let us play near his brook?" she wondered.

"Because he is mean," the other children answered.

2

Lucy read her book to Old Hook every day. One day, the children came to play at the brook. "Why doesn't Old Hook yell at us anymore?" they asked Lucy's mother.

"He's got a new friend," she said.

"Who?" the children asked.

"Peter Pan," said Lucy's mother.

7

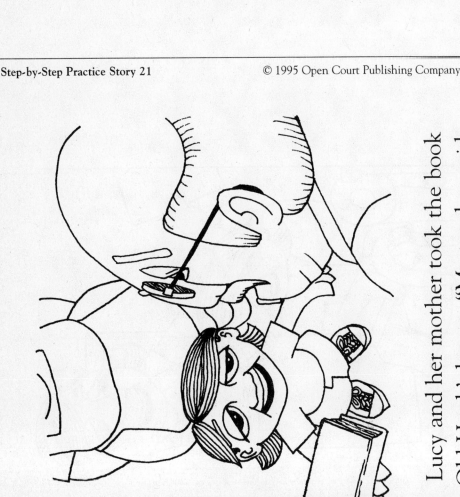

Lucy did not think Old Hook was
mean. "Why does he act like that?"
she asked her mother.

Lucy's mother said that Old Hook
was blind. She took a cloth and made
it into a blindfold. "Here," she said.
"Maybe this will help you understand
how Old Hook feels."

3

Lucy and her mother took the book
to Old Hook's house. "My teacher said
I need to practice reading. May I read
my book to you?"

"What book?" scowled Old Hook.

"*Peter Pan*," said Lucy.

"Hmm," said Old Hook. "Well,
okay . . . ."

6

Lucy tried making her lunch.
"It's hard to cook," she said.

Lucy tried putting on her shoes.
She could not even find her foot.

Worst of all, Lucy could not read.

"I don't know what I would do if I could not read books!" said Lucy.

Lucy took off the blindfold. She went to her bookshelf and chose a book. "This is a good book," she said, "I'll bet Old Hook would like it."

Lucy's mother understood. "Good idea!" she said.

The Proud Cow

by Dottie Raymer

illustrated by Robert Byrd

Once a brown cow named Flower lived on a farm just outside of town.

1

© 1995 Open Court Publishing Company

Scout looked around at the animals. They looked down at the ground.

"It sounds," said the mouse, "like some animals around here *are* too proud, . . . but I doubt that Flower is one of them!"

8

On the farm, Flower stayed mostly out in the field. She kept her head down, and never seemed to notice the other animals around the farm. The other animals thought that Flower was too proud to notice them.

Finally, little Scout the mouse spoke up. "Well, I don't know about plowing, or growling, or rooting, or laying eggs," she said.

"But I do know that you can always count on Flower for just the right amount of sweet milk."

When Flower was not around, the other animals talked about her.

"How can that cow be so proud?" Howdy the horse wondered aloud. "Why, she can't even pull a plow!"

"Root around?" pouted the hens and other barnyard fowl. "That's nothing to be proud of. However, if she could lay eggs like ours, now *that* would be something to be proud of!"

"Pull a plow?" howled Old Grouse the hound dog. "That's nothing to be proud of! However, if she could growl at prowlers, now *that* would be something to be proud of!"

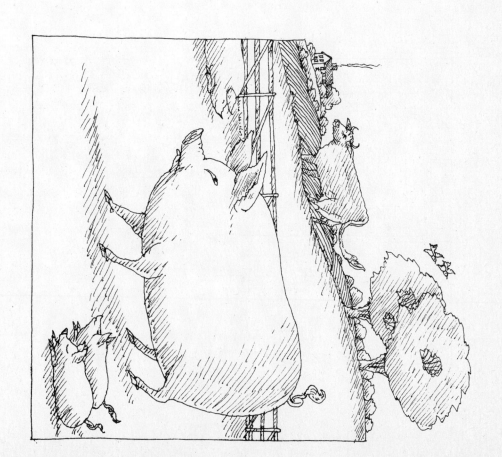

"Growl at prowlers?" shouted Stout the sow. "That's nothing to be proud of! However, if she could root around in the ground with her snout, now *that* would be something to be proud of!"

Aunt Maud's Pet Tiger

by Carolyn Crimi

illustrated by Ellen Joy Sasaki

Paul's aunt Maud had a pet tiger named Claude. Claude had four big paws with sharp claws.

"Claude is really quite tame," said Aunt Maud. "I have even taught him tricks."

1

"You found him!" said Aunt Maud happily. "You returned my pet tiger!" Aunt Maud gave the exhausted Claude a kiss. Then she turned to Paul. "Now can you help me find my pet lion?"

8

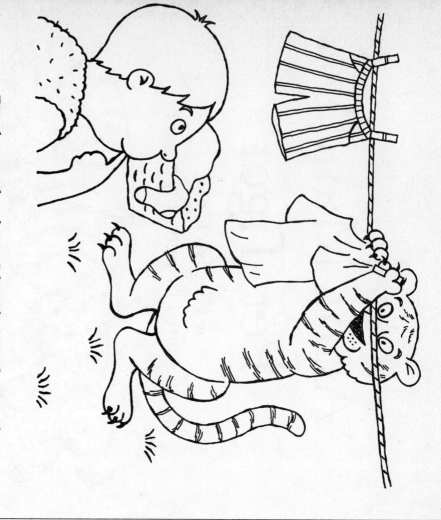

Paul watched as Claude performed his tricks. Claude could do anything! He could turn somersaults. He could balance on a seesaw. He could even haul groceries and do laundry!

"He must be an awfully smart tiger," thought Paul.

"You must be hungry, Claude," said Paul cautiously, "because otherwise you would never have caused so much trouble."

Paul gave Claude some sausage. Then, with a trail of raw cauliflower, he led the tiger back home.

"How do you get Claude to do these tricks?" asked Paul.

"I feed him well," said Aunt Maud.

"He likes to gnaw on sausages and raw cauliflower, and he loves to sip buttermilk through a straw."

"How strange," thought Paul.

3

Inside the store, the owner, Brawny Bill, was bawling like a baby. Outside the store, Paul saw an open box of straws.

"Claude must have been here, too!" said Paul. He followed the straws until he came to the playground. There sat Claude on the seesaw!

6

One day Paul saw Aunt Maud outside her house. She looked distraught. "Claude must be lost!" she said. "And everyone is too scared to help me find him!"

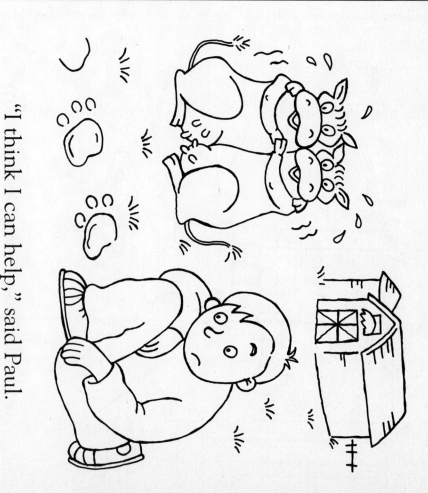

"I think I can help," said Paul. Paul ran across Maud's lawn to a dairy farm. "These cows look awfully scared," thought Paul. "I'll bet that's because Claude has been here."

He looked down and saw buttermilk paw prints. He followed the tracks to a nearby store.

Roy's Toy Store

by Zena Smith

illustrated by Joyce Audy Zarins

Roy has a wonderful toy store.
Customers are never disappointed.
They always find a special toy. I think
I'll go in and explore the store.

1

Well here is my choice. It's a bright
plastic coil that does all kinds of tricks.

8

What's the first special toy I see?
There's a shiny kite made completely
of red, green, yellow, and blue foil.
What a spectacular sight that would be
in the sky.

Picture just walking through.

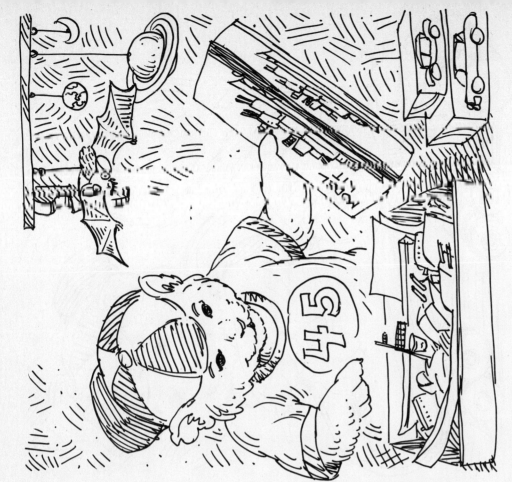

Now here's another fine choice. It's a model of a ship. It's a destroyer. Look at all the pieces. I'd need glue to join them all.

3

There's still so much more to see. There are games, books, and so many more toys. How can I choose?

6

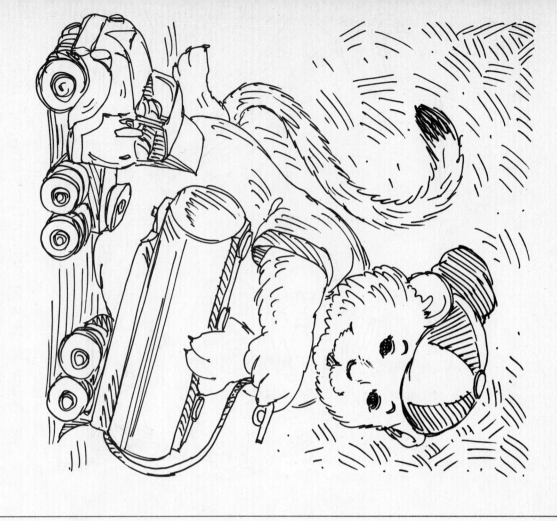

Next is an oil truck with a cab and trailer. They come apart. It also has a flexible hose.

4

There are shelves of dolls. They come in all shapes and sizes. Here's a princess in a royal gown. Another doll has a voice that almost sounds human.

5